LIGHTED DISTANCES

Also by John Daniel

Nonfiction

The Trail Home: Essays
Looking After: A Son's Memoir
Oregon Rivers (with photographer Larry N. Olson)
Winter Creek: One Writer's Natural History
Rogue River Journal: A Winter Alone
The Far Corner: Northwestern Views on Land, Life and Literature

Fiction

Gifted: A Novel

Poetry

Common Ground
All Things Touched by Wind
Of Earth: New and Selected Poems

LIGHTED DISTANCES

FOUR SEASONS ON GOODLOW RIM

JOHN DANIEL

BROADSTONE

Design by Larry W. Moore

Cover art quilt by Marilyn Matheson Daniel

Author photo by Alexandra Shyshkina

Robinson Jeffers excerpts courtesy of Stanford University Press:
The Selected Poetry of Robinson Jeffers, Tim Hunt, editor.

William Stafford excerpt from "A Ritual to Read to Each Other"
from *Ask Me: 100 Essential Poems*. Copyright © 1960, 2014 by
William Stafford and the Estate of William Stafford.
Reprinted with permission of The Permissions Company, LLC
on behalf of Graywolf Press, Minneapolis, Minnesota,
www.graywolfpress.org.

Broadstone Books
An Imprint of
Broadstone Media LLC
418 Ann Street
Frankfort, KY 40601-1929
BroadstoneBooks.com

For Roger and Karen Hamilton,
their clan, their land.

Contents

FALL

1

WINTER

27

SPRING

53

SUMMER

79

EPILOGUE

109

ACKNOWLEDGMENTS

115

I deal with the truths that recommend themselves to me ... A meteorological journal of the mind. You shall observe what occurs in your latitude, I in mine.

—H. D. Thoreau,
Journal

It is the job of poetry to clean up our word-clogged reality by creating silences around things.

—Stéphane Mallarmé

Southcentral Oregon.

Sagebrush-juniper country verging up into ponderosa pine forest.

The apron of Goodlow Rim, at 4,480 feet, looking southwest

over Langell Valley (soft "g") to Bryant Mountain, six miles out

and twelve miles long.

2019 – 2020

FALL

An aged man is but a paltry thing,
A tattered coat upon a stick . . .

—W. B. Yeats,
from "Sailing to Byzantium"

We should ask just how probable it is that a universe
created by randomly choosing the parameters will
contain stars. It is simple to estimate this probability.
The answer, in round numbers, comes to about one
chance in 10^{229}.
—Lee Smolin,
The Life of the Cosmos

Everything is the way it is because it got that way.

—D'Arcy Thompson

Morning is when I am awake and there is a dawn in me.

—H. D. Thoreau,
Journal

Arriving at night, headlights
    on the driveway gate—
        piled high with tumbleweeds.

Rimrock, valley, drifting clouds.
    I hold no deed, but all of it
        holds me.

In wetside woods I look up
    for glory. Dryside,
        I look out and far.

My view for miles—
    hayfields, pasture, sparse homes, barns,
        Bryant Mountain beyond.

Me? I'm on the page,
      I write the page, I stare back
            from the night window.

I sleep when I'm sleepy,
      wake when I wake,
            in daylight, in dark.

To welcome dawn and twilight,
      as in old Zen temples,
            I leave lights off.

~

Eight magpies.
      Five watch, three splash
            sumptuously in the small pond.

One whack with the maul,
    a crack. Whack the crack—
        juniper halves go tumbling.

The maple is shedding.
    I lug in firewood, crushing
        summer with each step.

The pasture trees,
    heavy with apples—deer
        rise on hind legs.

Merely to glimpse a wild critter
    eases some hurt
        I forgot I had.

Bully! Loudmouth!
    Don't hog the feeder, jaybird.
        What's so hot about you?

The three aspens.
      Yellow leaves quiver
            in a breeze I can't feel.

Sleek does drink and nuzzle
      at the pond. On my keyboard,
        a gray hair.

~

This apron is Goodlow Rim
      slowly weathering,
            crumbling toward the valley floor.

Junipers and sagebrush
      are my neighbors, amply spaced,
        agreeably quiet.

Junipers come straight-trunked,
        twisted, kinked, twin-trunked,
                storm-bashed, bushy, sparse, half-burnt.

Few graceful, each unique,
        hard-won histories
                where most trees can't grow.

Five stray cows rip grass
        by the pond this morning.
                Upslope, the deer watch.

Squirrel in the crabapple
        nibbles a sour fruit, too sweet
                to carry home.

Zazen. The I who breathes,
        the I who counts—
                have we two even met?

A prairie falcon
      lights at dawn on the dead spire
          of a juniper.

~

From the deck I see the grove
      at Pine Flat, where I lived
          forty years back.

My Eastern eyes found
      this dry country bleak at first,
          inhospitable.

But the spaciousness, the
      drama of clear distance,
          stirred my spirit.

I liked how the land
spoke in singulars—*this* tree,
that long sloping butte.

I tried to touch with words
the night sky, the smell
of sagebrush after rain.

The dryside seemed an open secret
that might lead me
to me.

~

Midnight walk, no moon, the sky
specked, studded, swirled,
jammed with stars!

Only a minuscule fraction, of course, of the roughly
hundred billion stars in the Milky Way, which in
turn is one of at least a hundred billion galaxies in
the universe.

No star in my sight or beyond is original.

After the Big Bang, as the gassy brew of the cosmos
cooled and darkened, some scientists believe that
enormous filaments of invisible dark matter formed
a cosmic web. Gravity, strongest at nodes where
filaments crossed or came close, gradually gathered
clouds of the brew, squeezing the densest clumps
harder and hotter until they flared with nuclear fusion.

So the first generation of stars was born. There was
light in the cosmos, seen nowhere, by no one.

Those shaky blue giants soon blew up, their matter
rejoining the cosmic flux as spacetime expanded,
stars blinked on in new galaxies, and galaxies gathered
in clusters—all loosely guided, perhaps, by the unseen
infrastructure of the cosmic web.

If the force of gravity were just a hair weaker, the
Bang might have yielded nothing but the gassy brew.
The slightest bit stronger, it would have produced
bigger stars that would have burned faster and died
sooner, before planetary life had a chance to evolve.

In either case, we would not have happened.

Time, matter, and the forces of Nature, without discernible intent, created a universe where life was possible.

True night is extinct
    where most of us live,
        but on the dryside, it thrives.

Bring children here. Tell them,
    You came of this bright heaven.
        You belong.

~

Twilight, harvest moon.
    A tractor growls. Geese fly, talking.
        I write these verses.

The long, pine-and-firred ridge
        of Bryant Mountain—
                my steady companion.

Splitting juniper
        cheers my spirit
                but earns me a stiff back.

Come spring I'll be 72,
        my father's age
                when cancer killed him.

If all day I remind myself
        to be mindful,
                is that mindfulness?

"Big sagebrush," it's called—
        this one stands six feet tall
                on twisting shaggy stems.

Crush some leaves, bury your nose,
     breathe deep—you only thought
        you were awake.

Wetside: Symphony
     in Green Major. Dryside:
         undertones, grace notes, solo songs.

No hidden thrush sings here.
     In open sky,
         a redtail's harsh whistling cry.

The night lights of Langell Valley—
     still a sparse constellation,
        forty years on.

Cougar who ghosted by
     the critter-cam last night,
        you saw my lit window.

I was writing,
     less sure of my direction
          than you were of yours.

~

Go, coffee grounds,
     onion peels, oatmeal glop—join
          the silent riot in the bin.

In town I go unnoticed,
     some gray-haired guy. No one gets it—
          I'm still a boy!

Where's the rain?
     Summer's bleached grasses
          sag with the sunny blues.

Ah, trapped spider,
      evolution
            did not plan on sinks.

The rut is on.
      Does mingle, quick-step uneasy
          around the pond.

Big buck lowers antlers,
      fakes a charge. Forked-horn
          turns tail. *Scoot, junior.*

Doe steps lightly away,
      buck plods after, down
          into junipers and dusk.

~

Seventy-four degrees,
      bare sky, November third—
         bad weather again.

To hike sidehill
      this apron studded with stones
         is an awkward honor.

Okay, I'm old.
      It was always in the future,
         now it's in the mirror.

How did all these years
      sneak up behind me,
         pressed so thin together?

Two bare aspens in the wind.
      The third still sounds
         a dry yellow chatter.

~

I trudge home off the rim,
        weary, heading downhill
                like the rocks. But faster.

No visitors this month.
        Me alone
                for distraction.

The fire I built woke you,
        bumbling wasp. Feels wrong,
                yet I swat you dead.

Zazen. I see my white skull,
        my skeleton
                in a loose black coat.

Death terrified me as a kid.
My life switched off
forever.

In my twenties I showed off
for death—motorcycles,
hard drugs, solo climbs.

But found a life then
in writing and marriage.
Death hung out elsewhere.

Now it's not so far away,
biding its time
as I spend mine.

Orion, old Hunter,
pierce me with your fierce fire.
I am not enough.

~

Town bustles, noisy
        streets, stores. Is anyone amazed
            that we exist?

I love those cheerful in their work—
        especially
                when I'm one of them.

City woman heard
        in a tavern: "Over here,
                I've got room to *fluff*!"

All day a clouded
        pewter sky, flooded now
                with blood-orange light.

Weaner calves bawl for their mothers.
　　When it's kids
　　　　at the border, we protest.

Bones, a husk of hide—
　　yearling deer, where
　　　　does your flesh roam now?

Contrails dissolve to hazy mist,
　　not dimming
　　　　the too-warm December sun.

Drippy day, and all night
　　I dream the moist scent
　　　　of sage and juniper.

A doe lifts her head—
　　drops from her muzzle
　　　　start ripple-rings in the pond.

~

Two inches overnight.
        It's cold, blank. Why does snow feel
            like such warm grace?

A truck's faint rumble
        climbing the Goodlow grade—
            a critter makes its living.

Tea leaves, Sumatran coffee,
        Mexican *chile* seeds—immigrants
            richen the compost.

Two quail at sundown
        poke downhill, flutter
            to their juniper roost.

Fly, I'm reading. You're buzzing.
    My mind's too small
        for you to get lost in.

Books for me, not screens.
    My fingers love the pages,
        the pages smell so good.

Coyotes yip and wail
    tonight. They feast,
        they sing, they rouse my spirit.

Done with decades of rooftop weather,
    these cedar shakes
        kindle my fires.

Juniper! Tangy scent
    hinted when you split it,
        supreme when it burns.

This tattered coat
      can still climb Goodlow Rim,
            split firewood, and write.

~

Walking the road past midnight,
    Christmas week,
          a brilliant scatter of stars.

Every birth of a human child, every birth of every
kind on Earth, is the latest in a long lineage—the Big
Bang, the first stars, the cluster of galaxies known as
the Local Group, and the second-largest member of
that group, our Milky Way.

In a spur off one of its spiraling arms, about four and
a half billion years ago, gravity worked on a whirling
disk of matter—a mix of debris from exploded stars
and the original gassy brew—and resolved it into a

yellow dwarf star of average size with eight or nine orbiting planets and countless leftover rocks.

The molten mass of Earth, pummeled by asteroids and comets, slowly cooled and crusted over. Epochs of rain made the oceans.

Probably in seafloor thermal vents, when Earth was still quite young, organic molecules somehow organized and learned the trick of replication. No poet, priest, philosopher, or scientist can tell us how this came about.

Yet, eons later, here we are, with at least an inkling of our story. Time, matter, and the forces of Nature, without discernible intent, produced a planet that readily gave birth to life.

~

Silver light suffuses
        gray clouds over Bryant
                as they let fall a shower.

The pond skinned with creased ice
this morning—a spider
begins an expedition.

One fawn, scattered bones.
Her twin stands by their mother,
eligible for winter.

Moonrise over Goodlow
sends juniper shadows
far downhill on frosted grass.

~

WINTER

Pull down thy vanity, it is not man
Made courage, or made order, or made grace,
        Pull down thy vanity, I say pull down.
Learn of the green world what can be thy place . . .

> —Ezra Pound,
>   from Canto LXXXI

I believe a leaf of grass is no less than the
journey-work of the stars . . .

> —Walt Whitman,
>   from "Song of Myself"

A little Madness in the Spring
Is wholesome even for the King,
But God be with the Clown
Who ponders this tremendous scene—
This whole Experiment of Green—
As if it were his own!

> —Emily Dickinson

What really interests me is whether God could have
created the universe any differently . . .

> —Albert Einstein,
>   comment to an assistant

Stepping out at night,
        tired of words—surprise!
            The soundless speech of snowfall.

Juncos splash madly
        in the thawed edge of the pond—
            what are they, Nordic?

Amber yarrow stalks
        stand swaybacked, on each seedhead
            a dollop of snow.

New snow comes drifting,
        slanting, swirling, *slamming*
            the windows now in gusts.

Stillness of junipers,
      boughs filled, a few
            fine crystals wandering down.

Hungry deer trample the snow
      for greens and peels
            in the compost bin.

Water heater died.
      Cold splash shocks my face,
            dirty dishes rise in stacks.

Henry Thoreau hated
      the telegraph. He would've liked
            a warm winter shower.

Old grasses I called bleached?
      Tawny now, some near russet,
            above white snow.

On skis I push and glide
        round and round the pasture—
            no thrill, great pleasure.

My three metal joints
        are the best I have, but once
            I'm moving, I'm good.

~

A thaw. Apron stones
        resurfacing
            look like black meteorites.

Underneath is older rock. Fifteen million years ago,
east from here, the stretched and faulting crust of
Earth spewed surge upon surge of fiery molten basalt,
at speeds up to thirty miles an hour.

A few million years later, Bryant and Goodlow were
born, mild volcanos emitting their own lava—the
source of my meteorites. As they rose, the block of
crust between them subsided and became a valley floor.

Just yesterday, the valley was an Ice Age lake that
might have been home to Asian hunter-gatherers,
whose recent relatives had either skirted the Pacific
Rim in boats or trekked the Bering land bridge and
followed an ice-free passage south.

The climate warmed, the ice withdrew, the lake
shrank to a slow river. The big critters of the
Pleistocene died off. Valley people had to adapt
their lifeways to smaller game and sparser forage
in the drying land. They would become known to
Euro-Americans as the Lost River band of the
Modoc Tribe.

One ancestor, who knows when,
        tapped human figures
                into Goodlow stone.

A few lines of people
        holding hands,
                very likely dancing.

How many seasons,
        their fire smoke rising
                in daylight and glittering night?

Their lives weren't easy.
        They knew wars, harsh winters,
                droughts, spells of hunger.

But they belonged to the land
        in ways we have lost—
                and might need again.

~

Snow flurries, sun gleams, then
        over Bryant, shafts
                of light pierce gray cloud.

At the pond, grown fawns
        nudge their mother to suck. She
            briskly steps away.

Snowstorm, tense driving—
        where does pavement stop
            and ditch begin?

Accident in town.
        We drivers idle, our fumes
            clouding the cold air.

I live away so not
        to breathe this, but I chip in
            my generous share.

Airplanes worse yet.
        We drive and fly, capsuled
            from the air we warm.

~

New water heater! I shower
        and shower. How soft I've grown.
                Not sorry.

Two prancing coyotes raise snow-sprays—
        they stop, sniff,
                bound on to the south.

Skiing Pankey Basin,
        behind Goodlow, so happy
                to have just two legs.

Sky, sun, snow—of all
        chances, how is it I'm here,
                this moment, this once?

How anything?
        The puzzle of puzzles, wrote Whitman,
            is that we call Being.

Cosmologists say Being came from a "singularity"—
our latent universe, infinitely dense, infinitely small.

This befuddles the laws of physics.

You could call it God. I call it Nature, which comes
from a Latin verb meaning *to be born*.

13.8 billion years ago the singularity gave itself birth
in a silent but very hot fireball, two billion degrees.

Time and space were born, as one. There was no
time as we know it before the noiseless Bang, no
space as we know it where the Bang took place.

So this odyssey began—the spacetime of Nature
expanding, incarnating its myriad forms, cooling
from its heated birth toward all it would become.

In the blue distances
        of snowy land this evening,
            stillness sings.

~

Critter tracks crisscross
　　　fresh snow this morning—news,
　　　　　but not the stories.

As I meditate,
　　　a mouse pauses
　　　　　at the toe of my left slipper.

Snowfall, muffled hush.
　　　Dark form glides above. Eagle?
　　　　　In a snowstorm? Gone.

Wild animals catch my eye.
　　　Of course.
　　　　　I used to be one.

Wolves, come home.
        The quiet of moon and stars
                wants your voices.

Reading in lamplight
        of the Buddha's wakening, I miss
                the dawn of day.

Errands in town, scurrying,
        I look up once—
                sunset, streaked with contrails.

This frigid night, the deer
        sleep beneath junipers—cold,
                yet not homeless.

~

The man who owns Pine Flat
        cut down every pine but one.
                Oozing stumps, busted crowns.

I lived there once.
        The wind told old stories
                in those tall ponderosas.

The bigger trees had orange bark.
        Their sprays of long needles
                glinted in sun.

Nature's gesture of pines
        defined that place before anyone
                owned land or trees.

This tremendous scene,
        wrote Emily, *this whole*
                Experiment of Green . . .

The Experiment made *us*
          just yesterday, and many think
               it's all *for* us.

The owner is not a bad man.
          Few are, but chainsaws screech,
               trunks slam down.

～

The stuff of the Experiment was forged, is forged,
in the superhot cores of stars. Starting with hydrogen,
atomic nuclei fuse, building the elements in sequence.

This process might have stalled at carbon, which can't
be made that same way. It took a fluky quirk of
physics called nuclear resonance for carbon to form.
Then came the other heavy elements, up the periodic
table to iron.

Passing through at least two generations of stars,
carbon became the chemical crux of life on Earth.
What Whitman intuited, astrophysics confirms: grass,
humans, all critters are the journey-work of stars.

That stars exist at all, that carbon occurs in abundance,
that the strengths of gravity and the other physical
forces are exactly what they are—if any of these or
almost any other basic characteristic of the cosmos
was the slightest bit different, life almost certainly
would not have evolved.

The odds of all these factors occurring together by
random chance? A flipped coin coming up heads
four hundred times in a row.

~

Crass sunlight scatters—
        so many *things*. Moonlight
                draws them together.

On full-moon walks
a dark wordless stranger
strides in step with me.

He could be the self I can't quite see,
because he's the one
who's looking.

I think the mind at night
seeks beyond thought the wholeness
from which it came.

Waters there move with meanings
hard for daylight mind
to understand.

The meanings matter, so
they rise sometimes
in the coded poetry of dreams.

Sparks and flames leap tonight
　　from my burn pile,
　　　　toward the stars that they once were.

~

Daybreak. Words won't say
　　how dark gives way to light, so I
　　　　keep watching.

I love these times between,
　　when boundaries form or fade
　　　　and mystery abounds.

Is mind inside the skull?
　　Mine feels *out there*, around
　　　　the dawnlit mountain.

What *is* mind, anyway?
    We pay more attention
        to our fingernails.

I see sky and ocean—
    an open vault of light
        over opaque depths.

The depths are mysterious,
    but still more mysterious
        is the light.

Neuroscience studies brain
    activity—mind observed
        objectively, from without.

But consciousness
    is mind *inhabited*, experienced
        first-person.

As the human brain, beneath awareness, constantly regulates our essential bodily functions, it is also shaping and organizing the information that comes to us through our sensory systems. How it performs these unconscious functions isn't fully understood but is coming clearer as research advances.

Consciousness is a steeper challenge. How do neurons firing in a three-pound mass of moist tissue give rise to our conscious ongoing *experience* of sensations, perceptions, emotions, ideas, beliefs, intentions, intuitions, memories—the impossible to express but very real feeling of what it is like to be alive as you?

Most scientists and philosophers believe that the brain does generate consciousness and research will eventually discover how. But another camp argues that consciousness, though it entails brain activity, is a further fact—something that cannot be reduced to chemistry and biology. They believe that even when the underlying functions of the brain are completely understood, they will not have explained the rich subjective realm of human consciousness.

But no mystery, say some.
Consciousness
is simply an illusion.

Well. Can't prove them wrong,
　　but my experience feels
　　　　as true as my toes.

~

I open my arms with love
　　but the deer just stare,
　　　　as if I've landed from Mars.

A fawn's black-and-white flag
　　goes up, black pellets
　　　　rain to the snow.

Some think DNA makings
　　did arrive from space—
　　　　in meteorites.

Carbon, oxygen, water,
   organic compounds—the cosmos
      teems with life-stuff.

Billions of planets in just
   the Milky Way, but life
      on Earth alone? Uh-uh.

Many suns in many skies
   out there, many worlds of
      distant relatives.

Let's hope they wait a while.
   We haven't even learned
      to converse with crows.

~

Rain, rain, melting the snow
        upcountry. Come summer
            the land will want it.

Langell Valley hinting green—
        grass, alfalfa think it's spring.
            Let them be wrong.

Dawn. Cottontail clips
        a grass spear, nibbles it up—
            a kid sucking spaghetti.

Dense white mounds of fog
        bury the valley floor this morning
            like tumbled cumuli.

Moonlight walk—small heifer,
        belly ripped wide. Spooked, I turn
            for home, clacking sticks.

Cougar, I'd be honored
      to meet you—in daylight,
          and not for a meal.

The fear that prey feel
      is enlivening.
          Mind clears, senses sharpen.

We'd feel it more often
      if our great menace didn't wear
          a familiar face.

Tonight a coyote cries
      the call of the wild. I
          sip my margarita.

~

Chickadee darts in
     for one quick seed
          as finches feeder-binge.

No valley. No sky.
     The dark pointed junipers,
          March snow softly falling.

Inside out, outside in.
     The snow drifts down
          without me, and within.

At twilight the stark
     black-tangled crabapple tree,
          limned in white.

~

Warm again, the damp ground bare.
    The first robins
        alight at the pond.

These fleeting days,
    I would take them in my arms.
        Slow down. Don't rush away.

Old Man Winter? Last seen
    trudging north in tattered furs,
        grumbling and sweaty.

Waking, listening,
    rising at will, the deer
        need nothing that is not here.

∽

SPRING

Beginning my studies the first step pleas'd me so much,
The mere fact consciousness, these forms, the power of motion,
The least insect or animal, the senses, eyesight, love,
The first step I say awed me and pleas'd me so much,
I have hardly gone and hardly wish'd to go any farther,
But stop and loiter all the time to sing it in ecstatic songs.

> —Walt Whitman,
> "Beginning my Studies"

The Brain—is wider than the Sky—
For—put them side by side—
The one the other will contain
With ease—and You—beside—

> —Emily Dickinson

I think the rocks
And the earth and the other planets, and the stars and galaxies
Have their various consciousness, all things are conscious;
But the nerves of an animal, the nerves and brain
Bring it to focus; the nerves and brain are like a burning-glass
To concentrate the heat and make it catch fire . . .

> —Robinson Jeffers,
> from "The Beginning and the End"

A distant throaty bugling . . .
       did I hear it?
               Sandhill cranes return!

High swirls of cloud
       shot through with hazy rays,
               rambunctious wind down here.

Whup. Seventy-one,
       and had to learn it again—
               don't piss into wind.

Social distancing?
       No problem. Junipers
               have done it for ages.

Flicker jackhammers
     under the eave, by the fake owl
          there to scare it off.

Packrat gnaws
     inside a wall, squirrels
          scuttle belowdecks. It's spring!

~

A spikehorn deer gazes downslope
     ten minutes, tail
          now and then twitching.

He waits for something?
     Lonely? Takes pleasure
          in sun, gentle breeze?

Who knows, but he's not empty.
      Being here, now,
               feels like something to him.

And why wouldn't life feel like something
      if you're a hawk, trout,
           snake, or bee?

René Descartes was confident that animals felt
nothing, not even pain. His followers performed
vivisections, explaining that the dog's yelps and
whimpers were merely mechanical, nothing more
than the sounds of a mill wheel turning.

Science took his cue. Three centuries passed before
the notion of animal awareness was deemed a valid
subject for research, and it wasn't until this century
that scientists broadly affirmed what hunter-gatherers,
farmers, and horse and pet lovers knew all along—
all critters possess some share of consciousness.

When the spikehorn lowers his head to drink from
the pond, though, he may not recognize his reflected
face as *himself*, his singular subjective being.

Researchers believe that some critters—crows, octopi, certain apes, whales, and parrots—do self-identify as individuals. Like us, they are not just aware—they're aware that they're aware. But those species, in turn, probably don't spend much time puzzling over the puzzle of Being.

We've got a whizbang mind, we humans, but it comes at cost. Our acute self-awareness withdraws us partway from Nature that made us and flows on around us. I write these verses about a given world I'm not all the way in.

There's loneliness in that, probably unconscious in most of us. I believe it eats at the human heart as we burrow deeper into our own creations and fixations, hungering for Nature even as we ravage it.

~

April ninth, 82
degrees, damp dead grasses
drying to tinder.

Spring's first mosquito
     drilled me in the neck. She died
       doing what she loved.

Ah, Nature. Big wasp
     eats small moth headfirst—
       wing-bits in the easy breeze.

Walk? Read? Clean house? Drink?
     Write a friend? Such dithering.
       Wild critters *do*.

Hope, fear, shame, joy, anger, doubt, sorrow,
     belief, love, grief, regret,
       confusion . . .

Self-awareness is *hard*,
     so mind drowns what it can
       in its bottomless gulf.

And bits bob up like flotsam
in obsessive thoughts,
bad dreams, bad habits.

~

Red-tail on the tall pine,
female. Now the male.
In seconds it's done.

Sometimes I feel
I've let Nature down.
I fathered no children.

Parents in my line
did not fail in four billion years
to reproduce.

Yes, we are too many.
    We overrun the green world
        that could be our place.

But I claim no virtue.
    I won the lottery
        and hoarded my good luck.

~

Up Goodlow today,
    desert buttercups blooming
        amid scree and boulders.

On the rimrock crest
    stand ancient junipers, roots
        clenched in cracked basalt.

Hefty green limbs swirl
from the sides of one tree, spire dead,
trunk six feet through.

Another, storm-slammed flat.
Living limbs grow straight up
from the splintered trunk.

Seed of these elders
scatters in wind, water, guts,
takes hold where it can.

The bristling youngsters
sink a taproot
longer than they are.

They rise sharp-pointed
like the ace of spades,
round their crowns in century two.

For centuries more,
      lower limbs fill out,
            the fat trunk leisurely swells.

~

Way down on Smith's pond,
      sober white pelicans drift, mute
          their entire lives.

Black angus dot green pastures.
      Far across Langell,
            one moving car flashes sun.

Clouds trail their shadows
      along mountain and valley
           like slow-passing thoughts.

Does it seem odd
　　　　to sense a kind of mind
　　　　　　　　in this lit vastness?

All things, says Jeffers, have a spark of psyche—trees,
rocks, the ash of supernovas. Science demurs, but
science, authoritative on the behavior of matter, does
not say what matter *is*. Particles do this, do that, but
what are particles made of?

Mind, conjectured Bertrand Russell, Sir Arthur
Eddington, and—separately—Teilhard de Chardin.
They saw matter as dual-natured—physical and
measurable from the outside, immeasurably conscious
within. Like us. Like any critter.

Proponents of panpsychism—mind in all things—
don't suggest that rocks can think and molecules
make plans (though somehow they *did* come to life),
but that the vanishingly small glint of sentience in a
grain of sand or an atom has scaled upward as Nature's
creations have evolved into greater complexity.

Modern views of panpsychism revive the intuitions
of the earliest Greek philosophers, who sensed gods
in all things, and Plato's later notion of *anima mundi*,
the world soul.

The Great Spirit revered in some Indigenous American cultures lives in everything, marking no line between what we call animate and inanimate.

And Buddhists, who've been exploring consciousness experientially for more than two millennia, have no trouble perceiving Buddha-nature in stones, rivers, landscapes, even the impermanent cosmos itself.

Rafts of cloud, lit pink
        underneath by the sunken sun,
            as I start down.

Boulders, brush, awkward footing,
      twilight just enough
           to see my boots home.

~

Along this dry apron,
        new grass pushes up
                through last year's flattened straw.

Two feral dogs stop by,
        sniffing. They earn their meals
                the old-fashioned way.

The Covid virus sniffs out
        human cells
                to highjack for breeding.

Viruses have plagued critters
        since life began. Their DNA
                is in our genes.

Bits of it protect the cells
        of growing embryos—
                from harmful viruses.

The body holds
　　in its inward sea
　　　　the history of its making.

~

Chickadee pecks one seed
　　held to a branch, wind
　　　　ruffling its black nape.

They were eggs dried
　　on birds' feet—now
　　　　three frogs yammer in the twilit pond.

But all three are hes.
　　Rough news for them
　　　　if there are no silent shes.

Squirrel crouched on stump
      half an hour in drizzling cold.
           That's meditation.

He might be in the moment
      I yearn for—*now*
           before I know it's now.

Original mind,
      broad and open
           as the cosmos itself.

Today he's on the deck
      munching sunflower seeds
           he filched from me.

Sitting upright, he cracks shells
      and spits debris as deftly
           as a baseball player.

~

Uh-oh. Drought, plague,
      bad governance—now a revolt
         in my own body.

Alien cells? Not at all.
      They are as *me* as the cells
         I live by.

A knife could excise them.
      Radiation could fry them.
            I could wait and watch them.

All praise to wildness,
      its ever surprising story,
            but this chapter sucks.

Gusty day. Maple and aspens
more spirited now,
all leafed out.

Cranes trumpet across far fields,
echoing ancestors
two million years back.

~

Juniper hole. A flicker
clings, tilts in and out, feeding
open craws within.

Two days later,
each parent in turn flies to the hole
but only stares.

What does worry
        feel like to a flicker?
                Or grief?

Now, each day,
        it's starlings
                in and out the nest hole.

Why am I repelled?
        Starlings rob nests, but I
                eat critters for dinner.

Nature grants
        the gift of birth.
                Full stop. No warranties.

In this dryside peace I love,
        coyotes, bobcats, owls
                rip living flesh from bones.

The cosmos itself
      was born and evolves through
          titanic violence.

Black holes eat stars,
      an errant planet bashes off
          the hunk of Earth we call moon.

Yet the Big Bang fireball
      finds voice this morning
          in a house wren's piping song.

And in these words too,
      this piecework I
          puzzle over day by day.

~

Bumblebees ravish the lilacs
  as butterflies
    flit bloom to bloom.

A thin white streak
  lines Bryant's backbone,
    the last shroud of winter.

The heifer that spooked me?
  Ribs, tattered hide. Stink. Flies.
    No death is wasted.

We too are food. In the end
  we owe what's left
    to Nature's many mouths.

Not yet though. I've hired
  a keen-eyed editor
    with a sharp knife.

~

The screen door bangs as I step out.
  Gray doves
    storm from the maple.

Mountain bike tips—aaah!—*crunch*.
  I'm fine, but this sage I crushed
    might be a hundred years old.

On foot now, hot day,
  breathing the sweet resins
    of ponderosa pines.

These trees play wind
  in a higher, more whistling pitch
    than wetside firs do.

The blackened furrows
      in their orange bark?
            Wildfires they've survived.

Open country now, buttercups, paintbrush,
      the rocky lookout
            over Miller Creek.

But what did *they*
      name it, those ancient ones
            who etched their lives into stone?

Five hundred feet down,
      the creek rushes white and green.
            Just a murmur up here.

I sing through stone,
      the murmur might say. *I called*
            you here. I know the way.

Long before any critter could hear,
this primordial voice,
this fluent tongue.

Mind and heart can know
just a pittance of what is—yet such
a fullness.

If we weren't human,
we would not sense the majesty
of the given world.

The mind that withdraws us can,
for moments, make us whole again
in awe.

Consciousness—a fleeting glimpse,
a bubble in the stream,
precious past measure.

As I head home, orange sunset
    promises no less
            than orange dawn.

~

Dense cloud bank behind Bryant,
    cresting its ridge
            like a breaking wave.

A seep of rain last night.
    The scrubby apron glows,
            moistly radiant.

Quail, your head-bangle
    looks ridiculous. But then,
            you're not courting me.

In the pond the lilies'
      deep green leaves unfurl, white blossoms
          peeking through.

Trotting coyote at first light,
      head, back, tail leveled—
          a spear of sheer intent.

Two yellow swallowtails
      flashdance together, in the breeze
         that bears them away.

∼

Summer

As we look out into the Universe and identify the many
accidents of physics and astronomy that have worked
together to our benefit, it almost seems as if the Universe
must in some sense have known that we were coming.

—Freeman Dyson,
Disturbing the Universe

Integrity is wholeness, the greatest beauty is
Organic wholeness, the wholeness of life and things,
    the divine beauty of the universe. Love that, not man
Apart from that . . .

—Robinson Jeffers,
from "The Answer"

His mind forebodes his own destruction. . . .
A little knowledge, a pebble from the shingle,
A drop from the oceans: who would have dreamed this
    infinitely little too much?

—Robinson Jeffers,
from "Science"

The more the universe seems comprehensible, the more
it also seems pointless.

—Steve Weinberg,
Dreams of a Final Theory

Deck zazen, dawn.
　　　　Such gab-chattering birds! For once
　　　　I'm the quietest.

Junipers shimmer
　　　　in noonday heat, a black shadow
　　　　pooled under each.

The American West is enduring its fifth megadrought
since the eighth century. This dry spell of more than
two decades is unique in that the habits of a single
animal species are making it worse. In a region largely
arid to begin with, winter mountain snowpacks that
once supplied summer water have dwindled with
climatic warming. Sunbaked soil hardens, creeks and

rivers shrink from their banks. Vast reservoirs fall
to record lows. Parched mountain forests burn readily,
for months. Summers grow hotter and longer. The
human population swells. Towns and cities, ranchers
and farmers, governing agencies, Indigenous nations,
activists speaking for ecosystems—all wrangle over
the fluid that life can't live without.

Junipers two thousand years old or more provide the
megadrought history, but their scrupulous records can
be hard to read. In drought their growth rings crowd
so close together, with such tortuous indentations,
that a section of trunk must be sanded again and again
with superfine grit before the rings can be deciphered
under strong magnification.

Five great extinctions
          in life's journey on Earth,
                    all caused by climate change.

Humans, self-styled smartest
          of critters,
                    are conducting the sixth.

Those who holler for growth,
          growth, ever more growth?
                    Please, take my cancer cells.

There is no place where
          plastic isn't. You're breathing
                    fine particles now.

A plastic-trash slurry
          twice the size of Texas
                    expands in the Pacific.

Air simmers, storms fiercen,
          oceans sicken and rise. People
                    sink into their screens.

Some might outright drown
          in VR blinders, absorbed
                    in the metaverse.

Are we trying to kill ourselves,
    or do we just not care?
        Is there a difference?

Human consciousness
    may turn out to be more
        than human beings can bear.

~

Look outward, Jeffers wrote,
    open the ingrown mind
        to Nature that made us.

Yellow balsamroots,
    bright lanterns of sun,
        splotch the upper apron.

First light reveals faint age-lines
      water has worn
            down Bryant's wooded flank.

June sixteenth. A one-inch
      white surprise this morning, gone
           by nine o'clock.

Eight young does
      around the pond,
           eight heads bowed to drink.

The mother deer
      lie in seclusion still
           with their spotted fawns.

Lizard on sunny rock,
      do you have questions
           for which warmth is not the answer?

~

My own summer mind
    too often goes slack, lazy,
        craving amusement.

I become a sump
    for distraction,
        refilling as it drains.

To be *distracted* means,
    literally, to be pulled
        apart.

It's wholeness of attention,
    outward, inward,
        that nourishes the soul.

Our earliest ancestor
        was single-celled
                and lived in water.

It had, perhaps, one simple choice—
        move toward sunlight
            or move away.

Eons from that glimmer
        to the human mind.
                Keep it fit, I tell myself.

~

Surgery soon. We nabbed it,
        my knife-man thinks.
                Likely has not spread.

Still, death snuck up
       and laid a hand on me, so gently
          I felt nothing.

Sometimes when I worry
       I sense a deeper self
          who does not fear.

To die is something better
       than we assume, Walt wrote—
          before he died.

On the ER gurney my mother
       reached one arm up,
          eyes raptly intent.

Around her, we watched.
       She could not speak
          her experience within.

Many species mourn their dead.
But does each critter know
that *it* will die?

If we didn't know,
would sunset or a lover's face
be as beautiful?

Could we love at all?
What would stir us
to sing, cry, tell stories?

Why do we die? Nature
says so. Why do we live?
You tell me, says Nature.

~

Blistering days.
      Smoke from California fires
            hazes Bryant Mountain.

Forty years ago
      the mountain burned,
            an awful glory in the night.

In this dry Goodlow cheatgrass
      a fire wave
            can outrun any human.

So can Covid. Bars reopen
      and the virus revels
            in the revelers.

Fake news, some scoff.
      Some scoff right to the cliff
            where Covid kills them.

A mask can block
          shouted spittle, but not
                    shouted hate.

Banding up once kept humans alive.
          The same instinct
                    rips us apart.

Wildlife heard today: a chainsaw,
          two shrieking fighter jets,
                    one fly.

~

Tiny owl *WHAPS* the window,
          twitches two minutes on its side—
                    and flies away!

Life does not inhabit Earth,
     it *possesses*—every
          height, depth, cranny, inch.

That fierce insistence
     has stuttered
          but never stopped.

Many species fewer,
     the Green Experiment will flow on—
          with us or without.

But how sad, what waste
     of evolutionary time,
          to self-destruct.

We can be so kind,
     so brave and giving, so
          superbly creative.

Humans are first on Earth
　　to wonder at the cosmos
　　　　and seek to know it.

We sense the beauty
　　of Being. But we can't seem
　　　　to *live* that beauty.

～

What greater delight
　　than a pondful
　　　　of flappedy-splashing songbirds?

The three frog brothers,
　　ever hopeful, still holler
　　　　their sparse evening chorus.

A crippled deer limps
southward, alone. Bad leg
can mean brief future.

Do junipers sleep? So keyed to sun,
somehow they must
waken at its first touch.

Trees communicate, we know—
root to root, and scent signals
through the air.

Intelligent behavior
does not require
brain or nervous system.

~

No trees today. No Bryant.
    A rank tide of stinging,
            throat-rasping smoke.

The sun, a lurid vermilion disk,
        looms like
                some alien moon.

A hundred wildfires
        across the West, whipping
                their own winds and weather.

Where lightning fires opened forest spaces, Indigenous
peoples saw game, berries, and medicinals thrive.

They started burns themselves, with great care fine-
tuning the land to sustain them.

Settlers observed. Some torched their dry pastures
in fall for lush spring grazing.

Then, for a hundred years, Smokey the Bear ruled.
Crews made war on wildfire. Some warriors died.

Even small slow burns were snuffed.

Forests reclaimed the clearings, stored up dry brush,
deadfalls, standing snags, and crowds of sun-starved
saplings. Suburbs spread into woods and brushlands.

So now, with drought and warming, come holocausts
of pent-up power. Big hot fires aren't new, but they
are more frequent now, some so intense they sterilize
the soil and bake it solid. More homes burn. More
residents and firefighters die.

Fire belongs. The land evolved with it. And so, as we
breathe the fumes of our own ignorance, we strive to
tame its ferocity by carefully thinning forests, catching
fires early, and burning as the first Americans burned.

But we are late to the task.

~

That Ice Age lake appeals
these late July days, the valley
an acrid swelter.

How welcome then—this
            air-conditioned
                        Portland hospital!

Less one unruly gland,
            I wake up cancer-free, a toddler
                        not quite toilet-trained.

Shedding anesthesia
            and the urban jangle,
                        to Goodlow again.

The smoke has thinned, but our sun
            burns mighty hot for a
                        four-billion-year-old.

Spotted fawn hops once,
            straight-up-straight-down—exclamation
                        on small soft hooves.

When the most depressed
       great horned owl on Earth
             drones its halfhearted call, I smile.

Magpie eyes jackrabbit
       across the pond, two outlaws
           thirsty for a drink.

So formally tailored in black and white,
       when the magpie walks,
          it waddles.

A fawn wanders
       upslope from the pond—not down,
          where its mother led.

The little deer does not smell danger.
       Nor did I. Safety
          is a spell.

But the lame deer
        is back with the herd! She limps, lags,
            but gets on.

Sun-silvered clouds stream above
        the calm valley,
                pushed, pulled, in a high wind.

~

The better we know the cosmos,
        a great physicist writes,
                the more pointless it seems.

Could it be
        he's looking for a point
                at the wrong scale?

Particles matter, sure—
        but who has ever admired
                or loved a proton?

It's the *creations* we love,
        the forms Nature conjures
                from the formless flux.

Stars, landscapes, living
        sensuous beings—maybe
                the cosmos *is* its point.

Science has peered deeply into Nature and unveiled much about its workings, but there are questions science can't answer.

Why a cosmos? Why *this* cosmos? Why are almost all its features biased toward life? Why are living beings conscious, and growing more conscious over time?

Why the universe exists may be unknowable, but the question is worth asking. Life and consciousness are

such profound realities, of such intrinsic worth, that
I sense purpose in their being. No orchestrating God,
no grand design, but a purpose immanent in Nature
itself, unfolding as the universe unfolds. I believe it
was inevitable that the cosmos would light with stars
and light again with conscious life.

Chance and accident are real. An asteroid six miles
wide ended the age of dinosaurs, giving a break to
certain squirrel-like critters who had scuttled at their
feet—and would, sixty-six million years on, become us.
If our ancestral story had been cut short at any such
moment, other lines would have evolved consciousness
as acute and complex as ours. Other lines appear to
be doing just that. Emergent life and mind are in the
generous nature of Nature, as fundamental to the
universe as atoms and gravity.

We think of purpose as pushing from a beginning,
but as Aristotle taught, purpose might also pull from
the end, the *telos*. Writing a poem or story, I don't
know the way it will take or what in the end it will be.
It shapes itself only as I engage the act of writing, on
the scent of a final wholeness I can't yet see that the
finished work may or may not attain.

I don't know toward what the universe is tending. It
may end in the formlessness of ultimate heat death, as
physics predicts. All critters die, Nature itself might

die, but transient Nature and our transient human lives are not therefore less meaningful. We are only beginning to understand our meaning. I believe in the journey of this universe, and I believe that embodied consciousness is crucial to its evolution. The purpose of the cosmos, in some still unconscious way, might be looking out through our own eyes, and the eyes of all the lives of Nature.

~

For our safekeeping we built a house—
  for us, our pets,
    and all our things.

The house sheltered us
  from wild beasts,
    but not from our own kind.

We lived freely, unconcerned
      with what we took from Earth
          or gave to it.

Floors sagged, walls cracked,
      but still we believed
          the foundation was sound.

The house tilts now, it quakes in wind.
      Seawater sloshes
          in the basement.

Many may die,
      but some who live
          might remember our true nature.

We are not random guests
      or hapless tourists
          on Earth for a quick ride.

We are a conspiracy
      of blazing stars, land and ocean,
            spiraling DNA.

We are old as time,
      strong as stalwart junipers,
            fresh as tomorrow's dawn.

We don't go into Nature
      or come out. We *are* Nature,
            its own awareness waking.

It matters, then, what we think,
      feel, say, do. We are vessels
            of what can be.

The petroglyph people
      held hands, danced, left their image
            to speak through time.

Any such mindful act
        can serve evolving Nature,
                no gesture too small.

Nature has all time,
        Nature has all chances.
                We have just this one.

~

Jackrabbit zig-zags hellbent *crazy*
        along the slope—chased only
                by my eyes.

Black bug stops, curls up
        at my pen's slight touch. Huh.
                I thought I was writing well.

Mornings come brisker now.
   The aspen tops
         are tingeing yellow.

Crickets pulse under evening stars,
      their gentle chant
            sounding the ages.

I'm melancholy,
      my richest mood. In one week
            I'm leaving Goodlow.

I will miss these lighted distances,
      to the mountain,
            to the stars.

But I love my wetside home
      as well, its spiring firs
            and misted fields.

That moist ground
>of fern and trillium
>>sometimes sprouts verses too.

Dryside airs and lights
>the spirit. Wetside freshens
>>the deeps of soul.

Joy and sorrow mixed
>stir me truest, like junipers fired
>>with sundown light.

∾

EPILOGUE

Farther along we'll know all about it,
Farther along we'll understand why....

> —W. B. Stevens,
> from "Farther Along."

For it is important that awake people be awake,
or a breaking line may discourage them back to sleep;
the signals we give—yes or no, or maybe—
should be clear: the darkness around us is deep.

> —William Stafford,
> from "A Ritual to Read to Each Other"

> ...unless
Soul clap its hands and sing, and louder sing
For every tatter in its mortal dress.

> —W. B. Yeats,
> from "Sailing to Byzantium"

At seventy-two
        I go on collecting days,
                grateful for each one.

This last evening
        I trek the apron
                visiting two favorite trees.

My boots crunch dry balsamroot leaves
        and spent sage stems
                silvering in dust.

An old juniper, lightning-struck
        against the rim, dead
                but for one green bough.

And a young one, slender,
        growing from a cracked boulder
            it will someday split.

My body will be earth
        by then, this borrowed mind
            gone back to its source.

Goodlow will keep crumbling,
        critters living lives—humans,
            I hope, among them.

Nothing here belongs to me,
        yet, like certain friends,
            I belong to this place.

Dry, rock-strewn country
        on a blue planet
            in a wilderness of stars.

I know little,
        but I know I am kin
                to all I can and cannot see.

I find my way
        the way a poem does,
                small wakenings one by one.

Life leads here, there, nowhere,
        always to oneself
                for the first time again.

I wait in stillness
        by the young juniper
                as dusk deepens into night.

A near-full moon
        lights the way home, shining
                like the open mind of darkness.

∾

Acknowledgments

Some of these verses first appeared in *High Desert Journal* and *Terrain.org*. My thanks to the editors of both.

Great thanks to those who read and advised me on the text: Wendell Berry, Simone Di Piero, Charles Goodrich, Joseph Green, Jim Hepworth, and Morgan Smith. For their encouraging spirit, I thank Steve Barton, Tracy Daugherty, and Paul Keller. John Laursen gave good advice on book design. And very special thanks to Ceola Norton, my dryside field correspondent in Summer 2020.

I did some reading and writing that led to this book during a residency at Playa, a fertile dryside arts community at Summer Lake, Oregon.

I was lucky to land my manuscript at Broadstone Books. Larry Moore and his team have been splendid in their dedication, enthusiasm, and boundless toleration of my quibbles and tinkering.

As ever, I am grateful to Marilyn Matheson Daniel, my first reader, for the room to write.

I developed my views on cosmology and consciousness mainly from these sources:

David Chalmers, *The Conscious Mind*
Teilhard de Chardin, *The Phenomenon of Man*
Paul Davies, *The Goldilocks Enigma*
Daniel Dennett, *Consciousness Explained*
Peter Godfrey-Smith, *Other Minds*
Philip Goff, *Galileo's Error*
Donald Griffin, *Animal Minds*
Donald Griffin, *The Question of Animal Awareness*
Thomas Nagel, *Mind and Cosmos*
Thomas Nagel, *Mortal Questions*
John Searle, *The Mystery of Consciousness*
Lee Smolin, *The Life of the Cosmos*
Frank J. Tipler & John D. Barrow, eds., *The Anthropic Cosmological Principle*

About the Author

John Daniel was born in South Carolina, raised mainly in the suburbs of Washington, D.C., and educated at Reed College, where he added psychedelics to the curriculum and washed out after a year and a half. He stayed in the greater Pacific Northwest, from the Bay Area north to Southeast Alaska, working as a logger, railroader, mortar man for a mason, rock climbing instructor, and breakfast cook before turning to writing as a last resort.

He bought a used Royal manual typewriter, a twelve-pound Webster's library dictionary, and sat at his table in Klamath Falls, Oregon, scribbling and typing. It didn't go well. His first published short story, in a climbing magazine, garnered $60.00 but contained 26 typographical errors introduced by the editor. His first poem in an environmental magazine was attributed to John David. A publicity photo in a small-town newspaper on the Oregon coast had the right name under it but showed the country musician Charlie Daniels.

When he heard that Dolly Parton had written a song about him, Daniel moved to an eastern Oregon ranch and focused on poetry. Wendell Berry and William Stafford responded to work he sent with candid but not dismissive criticism. When in his thirties the one-page lyric chafed his elbows, he took to writing environmental journalism and personal essays. As the essays ignited his memory in his forties and fifties, he wrote book-length memoirs. In his sixties, enlivened as a nonfiction storyteller, he wrote a novel. All the while he turned out a poem now and then.

Daniel has taught creative writing—poetry and prose—at Stanford, Ohio State, Saint Mary's College of California, Sweet Briar College, and St. Lawrence University, along with brief stints elsewhere. Poetry editor of *Wilderness Magazine* for twenty years, he edited *Wild Song*, the anthology of poems first published there. Through 2022 he was chair of PEN Northwest and administered the Margery Davis Boyden Wilderness Writing Residency in the Rogue River Canyon. He now sidelines as a freelance writing coach and editor.

Daniel's work has been honored with three Oregon Book Awards, a Pacific Northwest Booksellers Award, a John Burroughs Nature Essay Award, a Pushcart Prize, a Wallace Stegner Fellowship at Stanford, a research and writing fellowship at Oregon State University's Center for the Humanities, and a grant from the National Endowment for the Arts.

John Daniel lives on a rampant acre of tall Douglas-firs and vicious blackberry thickets in the Coast Range foothills west of Eugene, and spends time every year over the Cascades on the dry side of the state, where this book found voice. His wife, Marilyn Matheson Daniel, is a retired environmental engineer and active art quilter. The cover image of *Lighted Distances* is excerpted from one of her works.

A tech skeptic who does not own a cell phone, John Daniel is nevertheless as hooked into the web as anybody else. He can be reached at johndaniel48@yahoo.com and www.johndaniel-author.net.